John Cabot

and the Rediscovery
of North America

Explorers of New Worlds

John Cabot

and the Rediscovery of North America

Charles J. Shields

Chelsea House Publishers
Philadelphia

Prepared for Chelsea House Publishers by:
OTTN Publishing, Stockton, N.J.

CHELSEA HOUSE PUBLISHERS
Editor in Chief: Sally Cheney
Associate Editor in Chief: Kim Shinners
Production Manager: Pamela Loos
Art Director: Sara Davis
Director of Photography: Judy L. Hasday
Project Editors: LeeAnne Gelletly, Brian Baughan
Series Designer: Keith Trego

First Printing
1 3 5 7 9 8 6 4 2

Library of Congress Cataloging-in-Publication Data

Shields, Charles J., 1951–
    John Cabot and the rediscovery of North
    America / Charles J. Shields.
        p. cm. – (Explorers of new worlds)
Includes bibliographical references and index.
ISBN 0-7910-6438-7 (hc) – ISBN 0-7910-6439-5 (pbk.)
1. Cabot, John, d. 1498?–Juvenile literature. 2. North
America–Discovery and exploration–English–Juvenile
literature. 3. Explorers–North America–Biography–
Juvenile literature. 4. Explorers–England–Biography–
Juvenile literature. 5. Explorers–Italy–Biography–
Juvenile literature. [1. Cabot, John, d. 1498?
2. Explorers. 3. America–Discovery and exploration–
English.] I. Title. II. Series.

E129.C1 S55 2001
970.01'7–dc21

2001028274

Contents

Who Was
John Cabot?

I

On December 18, 1497, Raimondo di Soncino wrote a letter to the duke of Milan, a city in what is now Italy. The duke had sent Soncino as an *envoy*, or agent, to live in London. His purpose was to arrange business deals that favored Milan—and to keep an ear open for information. In his letter, Soncino shares news he has heard about a remarkable English sea voyage commanded by a fellow Italian, John Cabot.

7

In the letter, Soncino calls Cabot by his Italian name, Zoanne Caboto, and describes him as a gentleman who is "very expert in **navigation**." Soncino wrote that in May of 1497, Cabot sailed from Bristol, England, with a crew of 18 men. After stopping in Ireland, his little ship continued westward and slightly north.

After wandering for a long time, Cabot finally returned, claiming incredible discoveries. For instance, Cabot reported sailing into uncharted waters brimming with fish. The crew had only to lower a basket and pull up a big catch! Moreover, Cabot had sighted new lands, waded ashore, and claimed them for England. These new lands, according to Cabot, were excellent places and fairly warm. Perhaps even silk could be found there.

Then Soncino grows excited in his letter. He tells the duke that Cabot's first voyage was only the beginning. Cabot planned to sail even farther west until he reached an island called Cipango (Japan), "where he believes that all the *spices* of the world, as well as the jewels, are found." Cabot might be right, Soncino tells the duke, for provided the world is round and not too large, "the route [for spices] would not cost more than it costs now." The king of

England himself, Henry VII, had already offered to supply ships for Cabot's next voyage.

When he read this letter, the Duke of Milan must have wondered what John Cabot's thrilling discoveries really meant, if the stories were true. What strange places had he found that were not shown on the maps of the day? How did Cabot convince the king of England to put up large sums of money for sailing west and north from England in search of a spice route? After all, had not Christopher Columbus just pointed the way to the Orient by sailing west and south from Spain only five years earlier, in 1492? Was Cabot right in thinking that another route existed over the northwest top of the world?

We know now that Cabot had not reached Asia—just as Columbus had not—but had landed instead somewhere near Newfoundland. He then sailed south, perhaps as far as New England. This does not take away from his achievement. The success of his adventure took years of preparation. And the "new founde lande" he discovered in 1497 was England's first claim in the New World. Other explorers would follow Cabot's course to North America.

Strangely, little is known about John Cabot. Historical records and letters call him Zoanne, Juan, or

Giovanni Caboto. He was a citizen of Venice who moved to the English city of Bristol about 1494. We know more about his deeds as an explorer for England than about his earlier life as a merchant, navigator, and mapmaker. Who was the man who carried England's hopes of discovery on a small ship to North America?

Cabot's interest in new and different lands began early. He was probably born in Genoa–also the birthplace of Christopher Columbus–around 1450, which would make him about the same age as Columbus. One historian has suggested that the two men probably even knew each other.

A merchant like his father, Cabot traded in spices with the ports of the eastern Mediterranean Sea. Rare spices–ones highly prized in preparing food–plus silks and precious stones and metals, arrived in these ports from Asia. Eastern traders brought them either overland, or up the Red Sea.

When he was about 10, Cabot moved with his father to Venice, one of the busiest ports of trade with the Eastern world. Records show that he became a citizen of Venice about 20 years later, in 1471. By about 1482, Cabot was married to a woman from Venice named Mattea, and they had three

Genoa, a port on the northwestern coast of Italy, as it appeared in the late 15th century. Genoa was the birthplace of two great explorers: Columbus and Cabot.

sons–Ludovico, Sebastiano, and Sancto.

To improve his success as a merchant, Cabot learned navigation–steering by charts, maps, instruments, and the stars. Perhaps during these years, he imagined a new route to the Orient, as Asia was generally called. It would be a sea route rather than an overland route. On a business trip to the city of Mecca, where Eastern and Western goods changed hands directly, Cabot, it is said, asked Arabian

Europeans of Cabot's time desired silks, spices, and jewels from Asia. Until a sea route to the East was discovered, these items had been brought by caravans along an overland trail called the "silk road."

merchants where their spices and precious goods came from. No one knew, or would say.

As a trader himself, Cabot would have understood the reasons for secrecy. It cost less to purchase goods directly from their source. Any merchant who knew the source of the spices, silks, and precious stones from the Orient could cut out the traders who brought these goods to the Mediterranean—and could keep for himself the profits these traders normally made.

To his skills as a merchant and navigator, Cabot

added a third—mapmaker. He drew a world map, which mysteriously turned up in Bavaria in 1843. It has four parts that fit together, presenting a view of the known world in the late 1400s. Cabot wrote on the map in Latin, "This figure . . . contains all the lands . . . which have yet been discovered, with their names and the discoverers of them." The care with which the map was made shows that Cabot studied exploration closely. His knowledge of coastlines and *landforms* probably supported his belief that sailing due west from Europe to Asia might make for a shorter route than traveling east—the direction others were taking at the time.

But what of the dangers of long sea voyages west? Did people of 15th-century Europe, including Cabot, think the world was flat and that they might fall off its edge if they sailed too far? Actually, experienced travelers such as Cabot and Columbus strongly suspected that the Earth was round. Even ancient *astronomers*, navigators, and travelers noted that as they journeyed far in any direction, the stars would begin dipping toward the horizon behind them. This could mean only one thing—the surface of the Earth is curved. European explorers believed that with good ships and their skills as navigators, they could sail beyond the horizon and never risk falling off the "edge of the Earth."

After spending nearly 25 years in Venice as a merchant and mapmaker, Cabot finally decided to find a new route to Asia. Around 1490, a Venetian with a name resembling Cabot's appears in the historical records of Valencia, a seaport in Spain.

Cabot, like his fellow countryman Christopher Columbus, may have chosen to move to Spain for a key reason: he wanted to be on the *frontier* of exploration–the Atlantic Ocean. Voyages of discovery were sailing from ports in Spain and Portugal, one after another. Rulers of both countries wanted to find sea routes to Asia. Also, Europeans in the 15th century were very religious, and they wanted to spread Christianity to new lands and new people.

Unfortunately, however, neither Spain nor Portugal showed interest in John Cabot as an explorer. King John II of Portugal supported Bartholomeu Dias. In 1487, Dias led the first of several expeditions that rounded the tip of Africa. The Portuguese eventually reached India. In Spain, King Ferdinand and Queen Isabella rejoiced when their *mariner*-for-hire, Christopher Columbus, returned in 1493. Columbus believed that the islands he had found by

In 1487, the Portuguese navigator Bartholomeu Dias would become the first European to sail around the southernmost tip of Africa and into the Indian Ocean. This route would establish Portugal's right to an eastward sea route to Asia, forcing the sailors of other countries to look to the west.

sailing south and west were also part of Asia.

Cabot must have realized he would need supporters who were willing to think about other routes and new possibilities. So about 1494, he moved again, this time to the English city of Bristol.

He chose England, and probably Bristol in particular, based on his knowledge as a merchant. To start with, England was at the end of the spice trading line. By the time spices passed through various merchants' hands in Europe and reached England, their prices were extremely high. If he could sell the idea of a faster route over the narrow top of the Earth to Asia—England is farther north than

When he reached land after sailing west into the Atlantic Ocean for about a month, Christopher Columbus believed he had found the Orient. Cabot hoped to convince the king of England that a similar route to Asia could be found to the northwest of Columbus's.

Spain and Portugal—success would mean a whole new market for England in spices.

Also, Bristol was England's second-busiest port. Bristol merchants lived on trade, especially from fish caught in the waters off Iceland. From their dealings with Icelanders, Bristol merchants had heard of lands farther west. These coastlines might offer rich fishing grounds. Cabot could interest them in a voyage of discovery from that angle, too.

Finally, Spain and Portugal were rapidly claiming vast areas of newly discovered lands. Perhaps Cabot suspected that King Henry VII of England might welcome an experienced navigator with a bold plan to add a share of these lands to his kingdom.

Cabot must have been a man who could arouse people's excitement. Within two years or so of settling in England, he was on his way to see King Henry VII. His plan was fully backed in Bristol, where the people knew about ships and the sea.

On March 5, 1496, the king granted Cabot and his sons official rights to sail to all parts "of the eastern, western and northern sea" to lands unknown to Christians. (The king did not wish to encourage trespassing on Spanish claims.) Furthermore, one-fifth of any profits coming from the voyage would be paid to the throne.

Ferdinand and Isabella of Spain quickly protested. Columbus had already discovered what there was to discover, they declared. Their complaint came too late. After nearly 10 years of trying to raise interest in a new route to riches, Cabot had the king of England on his side. With the good sailing months of summer coming, he began preparing for his first expedition.

There would be three voyages in all: in 1496, 1497, and 1498. From the final one, however, John Cabot would never return.

The Lands Beyond Iceland

The rocky coast of Newfoundland juts into the Atlantic Ocean. John Cabot was not the first European to reach North America; the Vikings had landed somewhere on the coast (probably Newfoundland) around the year A.D. 1000.

2

There had been rumors about uncharted lands to the west long before Cabot proposed to explore them. Already in the 15th century, Bristol merchants ran a lively trade in the fish caught in waters off Iceland. From their dealings with the Icelanders, the English had heard of faraway places to the west. The Icelanders cherished their own tales about these places, too, especially about a fabled island called Frisland.

Even nearer to England, the people of Ireland proudly told the legend of St. Brendan, born in Ireland about A.D. 489. According to the legend, when Brendan was in his seventies, he and 17 other monks set out on a westward voyage in a *curragh*, a wood- or wicker-framed boat covered in sewn animal hides. The monks sailed about the North Atlantic for seven years. Eventually, they reached "the Land of Promise of the Saints." They explored it and returned home with fruit and precious stones.

Had St. Brendan reached North America? He may have. During the fifth and sixth centuries, Ireland was the northern center of Christian civilization. Irish monks went on sailing missions throughout the North Atlantic to spread Christianity. They reached island groups called the Hebrides and Orkneys (off the coast of Scotland), and the Faeroes (near Denmark). Perhaps Brendan had used these islands as stepping-stones to the area now known as Newfoundland.

In any case, the Irish legends about western lands probably reached the ears of yet another people: the Norse, or Vikings, as they are often called.

From their homes in *Scandinavia*, the Norse started raiding Ireland before the end of the eighth century. Their war galleys, known as longships, were swift and easily steered, perfect for quick hit-and-run raids. Going on such raids was known as going "i-Viking." It was by that name that the Norsemen became feared throughout Europe.

Sometime after 870, the Vikings settled in Iceland. But by 930, good farmland on that island had become scarce. When famine hit in 975, some Norsemen decided to move on. Perhaps the tales of earlier Irish voyages spurred them to sail west. In 982, the Norseman Erik the Red discovered a large island farther west, which he named Greenland. Three years later, a major expedition of several hundred people left Iceland and sailed to Greenland.

The Norse established nearly 300 farms in southeastern Greenland, split into two settlements 160 miles apart. One settlement supported 3,000 to 4,500 people; the other, around 1,500. These Greenland Norse were different from their Viking ancestors. They were merchants, not bloodthirsty sea-raiders. They used ***knörrs***, strong ships that were good for carrying cargo. It may have been while sailing in a knörr that a Norse merchant accidentally strayed west to Newfoundland.

According to Norse ***sagas***—tales about Viking

heroes that had been written down in the 13th and 14th centuries—a sailor named Bjarni Herjolfsson was making his way from Iceland to Greenland in 986. His ship ran into a severe storm, which blew him far off course. When the storm clouds lifted, he found himself near a strange shore. Instead of the icy mountains he expected, Bjarni saw hilly forests. This meant he was too far south. He sailed north for a week, until at last he reached Greenland.

Bjarni was a merchant, not an explorer. He had no interest in leading a voyage back to the forested shore. But 10 years later, Leif Eriksson, the son of Erik the Red, followed Bjarni's route in reverse.

In a sturdy ship, Leif and his men passed a land of rock and ice, which he called Helluland. This was probably Baffin Island, a large island to the north of Canada. Next, he found a country that was flat and wooded, which he called Markland. This was probably part of southern Labrador on the mainland of North America. Last, he reached a land that the sagas described as a place of grassy meadows, with rivers full of salmon. The area was hospitable enough to stay for the winter. Leif gave this land the name "Vinland." Leif and his men built sod houses and stayed a few months. When they returned to

Around a thousand years ago—some 500 years before Columbus and Cabot—Viking sailors explored North America, which they called "Vinland."

Greenland, they told of their adventures. Their descriptions inspired Leif's brother Thorvald to see Vinland for himself.

Thorvald located Leif's wintering place, but he was killed in a fight with local natives. The Greenlanders called these people Skraelings. They might have been American Indians or Inuit (Eskimos). Repeated attempts to settle in Vinland brought

Timber was scarce in Greenland. In fact, when Leif Eriksson returned from Vinland, he brought long wooden beams. Many of the later Viking visits to the area may have been to gather wood needed by the Greenlanders.

attacks from the Skraelings. Finally, the Greenlanders gave up and Vinland faded from memory.

Where was Vinland? Also, if it was any part of North America, why did the Greenlanders not settle other areas farther south—which were rich with resources—long before European explorers arrived?

For many years, historians believed that Vinland was an imaginary place that existed only in the Norse sagas. But that view began to change in the 1960s with the *excavation* of a Norse settlement at L'Anse aux Meadows in Newfoundland. Vinland, most experts now agree, was in North America.

L'Anse aux Meadows is a small settlement of eight buildings. Probably no more than 75 people—sailors, carpenters, blacksmiths, and perhaps slaves—lived there. Some women probably lived there, too. *Artifacts* uncovered at the site, such as a spindle *whorl*, a bone needle, and a small *whetstone* for sharpening, were often part of a Norse woman's everyday belongings. The purpose of the settlement may have been to repair ships. The site could also have served as a base camp for exploring further south. It isn't hard to imagine Norse settlers going off exploring during the warm summer months.

In fact, given the Norse custom of ranging far and wide, most scholars believe that Vinland probably was not just one place. It may have been a region that included Newfoundland and extended south into the Gulf of St. Lawrence as far as Nova Scotia and coastal New Brunswick. Supporters of this theory point to the discovery that the settlers at L'Anse aux Meadows grew butternut squash. This is a vegetable that normally grows further south.

This still leaves the question of why the Norse didn't move on to friendlier and warmer areas of North America. The answer may be that to the men of Greenland, Vinland was a

Although the Norse were probably the first Europeans to live in North America, their settlement never influenced people of other European countries. The idea of North America as a "New World" would have to wait nearly 500 years, until the time of Christopher Columbus and John Cabot.

These remains at L'Anse aux Meadows, Newfoundland, are probably part of Leif Eriksson's camp, which he established about A.D. 1000. Leif spent the winter here, then returned to Greenland. During the next 10 years, several other attempts to settle in Vinland failed.

distant place. Their sagas describe sailing there as risky and uncertain. Also, the Norse expeditions met with hostile people whose weapons were as advanced as those of the Norse. The small bands of Vikings who tried to gain a foothold in America were no match for their enemies.

More important, at that time in the early 11th century the Greenland Norse settlements were still young. The land was hard to farm and the settlers struggled to survive. They didn't have the material goods to start up again in another land. The situation never improved, either. By the 14th century, hunger stalked the Norse settlements, the thin soil for farming having been stripped away. By Cabot's day in the late 1400s, the Greenland settlements were deserted. Vinland became one of the fabled places known to storytellers but never visited by any living European.

So the Norse exploration of North America, though by far the earliest for which we have definite proof, left only a faint mark in history. On the other hand, the voyages of John Cabot provided England with its first step toward exploring—and eventually settling—a "new founde lande."

A replica of the Matthew *sets sail from Bristol on May 4, 1997, to mark the 500th anniversary of Cabot's voyage to North America.*

Cabot's First Two Voyages 3

When King Henry VII granted Cabot official rights to sail west in March 1496, the best time for such a sea journey from England–April and May–was rapidly approaching. Cabot made his first try that same year. The voyage was a failure. Perhaps he needed more time to prepare.

All that is known about Cabot's first voyage appears in a 1497 letter from John Day, an English explorer and merchant who traded with Spain. The letter, found in 1956, is addressed to a "Lord Admiral"–probably Christopher Columbus. Day writes, "[Cabot] went with one ship, he had a disagreement with the crew, he was short of food and ran into bad weather, and he decided to turn back."

Running short of food may be a sign that Cabot had indeed left too soon. That mistake, added to a second-rate crew, would have been too much bad luck for a wise captain. Cabot headed back to Bristol.

On the other hand, an event during this failed voyage in 1496 may have helped Cabot's second expedition succeed in 1497. An old Icelandic folk tale says someone in a large vessel from Bristol visited Iceland. He was "a Latin man," meaning a person who spoke Spanish, French, or Italian. His fine manners, his great learning, and his ideas about geography impressed the Icelanders who met him. This "Latin man" wished to know about the western lands the Icelanders had discovered, explored, or settled. He was given all possible help. Then he sailed away. The following summer, he returned on a small ship with a small crew.

Could this "Latin man" have been Cabot? If so, perhaps Cabot learned everything he could from the Icelanders in 1496. Then he might have returned the next summer to pick an experienced Icelandic *pilot*, or steersman, to help him sail west.

On May 20, 1497–the summer after his first attempt–Cabot set out from Bristol again.

We don't know whether he had the same ship at his command, but the records show that the *Matthew*, a small two-masted ship, made the second voyage. Cabot's son Sebastian, who was also destined to become a famous explorer, went with his father on this trip.

As a Venetian, Cabot would have recognized a good ship when he saw one. Venice's shipyards worked like assembly plants, with cranes and other machines bringing large parts of a ship together. English shipbuilding was simpler. The builder chose a smooth bank at the water's edge so the finished ship would be easy to slide in for launching. Big wooden blocks set in two lines held the ship upright as it was constructed.

English shipbuilding may have been basic, but the materials used were excellent. The frame and **keel** of a Bristol ship like the *Matthew* would have been made of oak, chosen for its strength. Oak trees

Ships were often named for Christian saints or religious figures. Cabot's choice of Matthew followed that tradition. However, it is said that he really named the ship for his wife, Mattea.

were plentiful in England then. The side planks and deck would be pine, best for flexing under the weight of waves and for shedding water. Iron clamps appeared in a few places, but long wood pegs served as bolts everywhere. Driven into hand-drilled holes, the pegs swelled when wet, holding as tight as metal. The treelike *spars* that held the sails aloft were made of spruce fir that was hundreds of years old so it had the right thickness. The grayish sails were made of flax, a natural fiber, or cut from canvas imported from Europe.

To keep the ship watertight, workmen filled the spaces between the planks with oakum, a hairy cord made from the tough fiber of a plant called *hemp*. Their hammers rang loudly as they drove it deep into cracks. Next, the workmen sealed every inch of oakum and the entire *hull* with black tar or pitch. Then the rigging, or ropes, about the ship were added. Finally, the decks and rails received coats of colorful green, blue, yellow, and red paint.

On the day of launching, a priest would say a prayer and sprinkle holy water on the ship's *bow*. Just for luck, though, the shipbuilder had already made sure a shiny coin rested under the foot of the main mast where it sat on the keel.

This colored woodcut is from an Italian book on shipmaking that was published in 1486. It shows a galley being constructed in a Venetian shipyard. English shipbuilding was not as advanced in Cabot's day, but the English did turn out solid ships, like the Matthew.

From end to end, a ship like the *Matthew* would be from 54 to 60 feet long. It would have two decks: the main deck below for storing supplies, and the spar deck, which was open to the weather. The head room between them was 5 feet or less. The sailors slept wherever they could find a comfortable spot.

A view of the spar deck of the Matthew, *a reconstruction built in the 1990s to commemorate Cabot's voyage. This ship is on display at Cape Bonavista, Newfoundland.*

The only people who had bunks were the officers. These included the captain; the **boatswain**, who gave the captain's orders to the crew and was in charge of the ship's hull; and the ship's carpenter, who kept the ship in good repair.

The mariners supplied their own clothes. The usual outfit consisted of loose trousers, woolen socks, and a kind of long jacket with a hood. The sailors dressed in bright colors such as red or blue. They usually wore the same clothes all the time, causing one writer to complain about the "nasty beastliness" of the smell. They wore shoes, too, but mostly the sailors went barefoot because leather on wet decks is slippery.

With a crew of 18 aboard the *Matthew* (probably a different crew from the one on the unsuccessful first voyage), Cabot began his second voyage of discovery from Bristol on May 20, 1497.

The *Matthew* sailed slowly from Bristol down the Avon River, which leads to the sea. A few churches may have rung their bells in farewell. Bristol tradition says a local pilot went on the voyage with

Supplies were stored on the covered main deck of the Matthew. *Cabot's ship was probably about 54 feet long and carried a crew of 18 sailors.*

Cabot. But it's more likely that he only guided the ship around the dangerous Horseshoe Bend in the river, then went ashore at Avon-mouth. From there, the open ocean lies dead ahead.

Once at sea, discipline was probably the order of the day, every day. Although there are no records to show what life was like on the *Matthew*, historians do know about the practices on other ships during this time. For example, when John's son Sebastian became captain of his own ship, he ordered his crew not to offend God by swearing, telling dirty stories, or gambling. He insisted on morning and evening prayers and hymn singing at dawn.

Punishment on ships was harsh. For instance, a cabin boy who upset the navigation figures by failing to turn the hourglass over every half hour received a whipping from the boatswain. A lazy mariner ran the risk of being pinned to the main mast for hours by a dagger through his hand. Another who argued too much might be held by his ankles and dunked headfirst in the chilly water. Plots to ***mutiny***, or take over command—the worst crime aboard a ship—were punishable by keelhauling. Keelhauling meant shoving a mariner over the bow and dragging him by a rope around his waist underwater the entire length of the ship to the **stern**. The hard-shelled barnacles on the belly of the ship cut like razors. Some mutineers did not survive this punishment.

The food on the ship affected the mariners' moods, of course. Most ships allowed each man a pound of biscuit, a quarter pound of butter, a half pound of cheese, a pound of pickled beef or pork, a little honey, and a gallon of beer per day. On Fridays and other Catholic holy days, dried codfish replaced the beef or pork. Mariners could always catch fresh fish as well.

As the sailors hoisted the sails and worked around the ship, they may have sung chants like this one:

Ho, ho, ho–
Pull a', pull a'
bowline a', bowline a',
darta, darta,
hard out stiff
before the wind,
God send, God send
Fair weather,
fair weather,
Many prizes,
many prizes
God fair wind send
stow, stow
make fast and belay!

A constant sore point was the biscuit, or hard bread. The mariners needed it for strength, but the dampness of the ship made it moldy. Eggs that insects had laid in the flour hatched and became

Inedible food was common on long sea journeys. Christopher Columbus's son Ferdinand wrote about the disgusting fare on his father's fourth voyage: "What with the heat and dampness, our ship biscuit had become so wormy that, God help me, I saw many who waited for darkness and to eat the porridge made of it, that they might not see the maggots; and others were so used to eating them that they didn't even trouble to pick them out because they might lose their supper."

wormlike maggots. Warmer weather also brought out cockroaches and rats.

Nothing was heard of Cabot and the *Matthew* after the ship left Dursey Head, Ireland, two days after sailing from Bristol on May 20. Dursey Head was the last dependable point of land west. Beyond that, the ocean turned into a strange, uncharted area. Some mapmakers drew monsters' faces on the large uncharted spots to hide their ignorance of what lay there. For 11 weeks, the families of the *Matthew*'s crew waited.

Then, on the evening of August 5, the *Matthew* appeared quietly again at Avon-mouth, waiting for the tide to carry it on into Bristol. The next morning, August 6, 1497, the ship docked at Bristol Bridge and the crew leaped happily into the arms of friends, family, and sweethearts.

Cabot, hardly waiting to tell his tale, left the same day on horseback for London. He had news that no other man had the right to tell the king of England—that he had succeeded in planting England's flag on a shore unknown to all Europe. Better still, he believed he had found the beginning of a new route to Asia.

Cabot's "New Founde Lande"

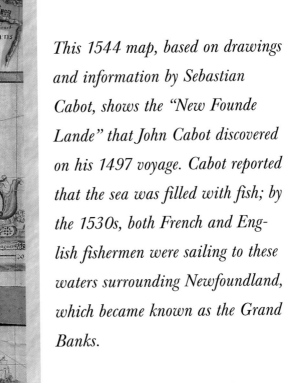

This 1544 map, based on drawings and information by Sebastian Cabot, shows the "New Founde Lande" that John Cabot discovered on his 1497 voyage. Cabot reported that the sea was filled with fish; by the 1530s, both French and English fishermen were sailing to these waters surrounding Newfoundland, which became known as the Grand Banks.

4

C abot arrived in London at the court of King Henry VII on August 10, 1497, just four days after landing safely in Bristol. The distance from Bristol to London is 130 miles, so Cabot must have ridden hard by horseback to arrive that quickly. No doubt he was eager to tell his news and receive a reward. His three sons, mentioned in the king's official letter of permission, may have accompanied their proud father.

The meeting with the king went well. News of it spread throughout the city. Rumors flew that Cabot had discovered a route to the kingdom of the Great Khan in central Asia. This was China, which Marco Polo had written about some 200 years before. A Venetian living in London, Lorenzo Pasqualigo, wrote to his brothers on August 23:

> Our Venetian, who went with a small ship from Bristol to find new islands, has come back. . . . He has been away three months on the voyage. . . . This king has been much pleased. . . . The king has promised for another time, ten armed ships as he desires, and has given him all the prisoners, except such as are confined for high treason, to go with him, as he has requested; and has granted him money to amuse himself till then. Meanwhile, he is with his Venetian wife and his sons at Bristol.

It may seem odd that the king would promise Cabot prisoners as crewmen on a third voyage, or that Cabot would even want them. It must be remembered, however, that finding crews to fill several ships on a dangerous journey would be hard. Prisoners were more likely to volunteer, first to enjoy freedom, and second in the hope that they might come into money somehow.

England had fallen behind other European powers in exploration when King Henry VII gave Cabot permission to seek the northern passage to Asia in 1496.

Lorenzo Pasqualigo says the king awarded Cabot money, but he does not say how much. The royal book of expenses says the amount was £10 (the pound, or £, is the English monetary unit comparable to the American dollar) "to hym that founde the new Isle." This was equivalent to about half a year's average salary. This was not very generous, but the king also promised Cabot an annual *pension* of £20, which would keep him comfortable for life. In January 1498 another note in the king's record book says a "rewarde" of a small amount of money was given "to a Venysian [Venetian]"–probably Sebastian, for accompanying his father on the voyage.

With his sudden fame, Cabot happily plunged into the role of acting like a great man. Pasqualigo says Cabot dressed himself in expensive silk clothes. People began calling him the Great Admiral. He was a celebrity in the streets. When he returned home to Bristol, Cabot rented a house on a street named for St. Nicholas, the patron saint of sailors.

No record exists of what Cabot actually told the king about his voyage (the king himself later began using the phrase "the new founde lande"). Also, neither a map nor a globe made by Cabot exists to show his route to that land. Letter writers of the day have filled in some of the details of what happened to Cabot and the crew of the *Matthew* during their 11-week voyage between May 22 and August 6, 1497. But their "facts" tend to be confusing.

Raimondo di Soncino, the envoy from Milan living in London, wrote to the duke of Milan that Cabot left Bristol, rounded Ireland, and turned northward, finally turning to the west and "leaving the north on his right hand after some days." This rough but clear description means that Cabot headed toward North America. Pasqualigo wrote his brothers that Cabot "says he has discovered mainland 700 leagues away, which is in the country of the

Great Khan." As a measure of distance, a league at sea is a little more than three miles. Therefore, Pasqualigo puts Cabot's sailing distance to a mainland at about 2,100 miles. By contrast, an unsigned letter to the duke of Milan stated that Cabot "has also discovered the Seven Cities, 400 leagues from England." At the Spanish court, Pedro de Ayala told King Ferdinand and Queen Isabella, "I believe the distance is not 400 leagues." Finally, the English merchant John Day wrote to Columbus that "the cape nearest Ireland [in the New World] is 1,800 miles west of Dursey Head." This figure fits better with estimates of 700 leagues or 2,100 miles.

The eastern coast of North America is irregular, so it's impossible to say which estimate is closest to the actual distance Cabot traveled. Likewise, no one can say for sure where Cabot first sighted land.

One person who should have known was Cabot's son, Sebastian. A map, copied from a drawing by Sebastian, carries the date 1544. Next to what is now called the island of Cape Breton appear the words "the first land seen." In the margin there is also a statement in Spanish and Latin saying, "This country was discovered by John Cabot, a Venetian, and Sebastian Cabot, his son."

John Cabot's son Sebastian was also a noted explorer. Under the English flag, he returned to the coast of North America in 1509, sailing into what later became known as Hudson's Bay. After this, he joined the service of Spain, exploring the coast of South America in 1526.

Can the map be trusted? If Sebastian drew the original many years after his father's voyage, he might have been guessing about the *Matthew's* **landfall**. First of all, John Cabot and his crew, gazing from the deck, would have seen nothing familiar to establish where they were. Second, in 1544 Sebastian could have been assisting English claims to North America by choosing a good spot on the map.

Here is how many historians reconstruct John Cabot's voyage to North America. The *Matthew* was a fast, well-made, and seaworthy ship. On May 20, 1497, it departed Bristol with a crew of 18. Like Columbus, Cabot decided to cross the ocean at a specific distance north of the equator. This would make navigating easier. He chose the latitude of Dursey Head, Ireland, and plotted out a north-western course along it. This heading was much farther north than Columbus's route, and well out of the way of Spanish-held territories. Two days later, he rounded Dursey Head and continued westward along this line of latitude, arcing slightly north.

By following this course, Cabot believed he would touch the northeast corner of Asia, maybe the legendary Cathay (China). Then, turning south-east, he would eventually reach Cipango (Japan). From there he would continue south to India. He probably wasn't certain at which latitude he would find Cipango or India, but in terms of longitude, he knew they must be west of the lands Columbus had discovered. Anyone who had read Marco Polo's lush descriptions of his travels in the Orient—which Cabot certainly had—knew that Columbus's landfall of deserted beaches and sparse jungle could not be the realms of the Great Khan.

Perhaps the *Matthew* dropped anchor for a day or two in Iceland to pick up a pilot. Continuing on, Cabot probably showed no interest in Greenland. He knew of it, either from Bristol fisherman or from

Icelanders, if indeed he had visited Iceland during the summer before.

By now, Cabot and his crew had been heading northwest for almost a month. On June 21 or 22, they ran into a storm. In fact, because of the unfavorable weather in the north, Cabot's journey would take him longer than Columbus's, even though the overall distance to landfall was shorter.

About dawn on June 24, a rugged coast poked above the dim horizon, 12 to 15 miles away. American historian Samuel Eliot Morison, an admiral in the United States Navy, argues convincingly that it was Newfoundland and, by coincidence, only five miles away from where Leif Eriksson had stepped ashore on what the Norse called Vinland.

Following his plan, Cabot then turned south, searching for a suitable harbor to drop anchor and claim the land for England. Turning north may not have been possible for a simple reason: ice. As late as June, icebergs and ice floes still drift in the waters where the *Matthew* lay offshore. Their tremendous weight could easily have crushed the *Matthew*'s wooden hull.

Once he sighted a harbor, Cabot, being an experienced mariner, would have sent in the small ship's

The Matthew *replica sails within sight of Newfound-land. No one is certain of the exact route Cabot took to reach North America.*

boat to test the holding ground of the harbor's floor. If the bottom was hard stone or slippery, the anchor would fail to grip, and the *Matthew* might drift away. Next, Cabot probably assigned roles for the landing party. Some crewmen would take weapons from their racks–crossbows, cutlasses or broad swords, and pikes, which were sharpened iron poles. The remaining men would carry either an English flag or a cross that could be raised.

From this point, we have John Day's description in his letter to Columbus. Day seems to have talked to a crew member, or perhaps to Cabot himself:

> [H]e landed at only one spot of the mainland, near the place where land was first sighted, and they disembarked there with a crucifix and raised banners with the arms of the Holy Father and those of the King of England, my master; and they found tall trees of the kind masts are made, and other smaller trees and the country is very rich in grass. In that particular spot, as I told your Lordship, they found a trail that went inland, they saw a site where a fire had been made, they saw manure of animals which they thought to be farm animals, and they saw a stick half a yard long pierced at both ends, carved and painted with brazil [reddish purple], and by such signs they believe the land to be inhabited.

Day says that because the men were so few and not heavily armed, they dared not go farther inland. As proof that the land was inhabited, they collected fish nets and snares. Then they climbed back into the ship's boat and rowed back to the *Matthew*. Sailing along the shore, they saw "fields where they thought might also be villages, and they saw a forest whose foliage looked beautiful." They also spotted two figures chasing each other, "but they could not tell if they were human beings or animals."

Cabot continued exploring the coastline, naming

the features he encountered Cape Discovery, Island of St. John, St. George's Cape, the Trinity Islands, and England's Cape. These may be, in order, the present Cape North, St. Paul Island, Cape Ray, St. Pierre and Miquelon, and Cape Race, all in the area of what would many years later be named Cabot Strait. How far south he sailed, no one knows. Perhaps it was as far as New England–but finding the water getting deeper, Cabot believed the land would soon turn to the west so that he could sail to the Orient. The crew hauled up plenty of fish too. Cabot was pleased. He knew that he could tell the king that England would no longer have to depend on Iceland for fishing grounds.

But with the season of good sailing weather growing short, and food no doubt running low, Cabot turned for home about July 20. Only one small mishap occurred on the speedy return voyage. The *Matthew* sailed to the coast of France, instead of England. After two more days of sailing almost straight north, Cabot's crew arrived at the mouth of the Avon River, which carried them triumphantly into Bristol.

It was August 6, 1497.

Lost at Sea
Forever

A memorial to John Cabot looks out over the Atlantic Ocean near Cape Bonavista, Newfoundland. Although it would be nearly a century before England followed up on Cabot's discovery by attempting to settle Newfoundland, his voyages mark the start of England's development into a seafaring power and the master of a colonial empire.

5

Although Henry VII received Cabot warmly in London, some fisherman in Bristol grumbled that the foreigner from Venice had found nothing. They said they already knew about his "new founde lande."

But none of this dampened the enthusiasm of the king. Despite the fact that Cabot had produced no jewels, gold, or spices from his voyage—just fish nets and a humble painted stick—on February 3, 1498, Henry granted new letters of permission "to our well beloved John Kaboto, Venician" to undertake a third voyage. This time the expedition Cabot assembled was impressive. The king financed one ship, and Bristol merchants paid for another four, which were stocked with trade goods they hoped would appeal to strangers: caps, lace, cloth, and "other trifles." Three hundred men signed on to crew the ships.

At the beginning of May 1498 the little *flotilla* sailed away. Sebastian was not on board.

They first went north. Cabot probably wanted to make certain that there wasn't a passage lying farther above where he had sighted land on the previous trip. Not long after departing, one of the five ships returned to Ireland, badly beaten by the weather. The other ships never returned.

It is believed that Cabot reached Greenland in June. He then sailed northward along the coast. The crew may have mutinied because of the severe cold, forcing Cabot to turn south. He may then have cruised along the coast of North America to Chesapeake Bay or Cape Hatteras. If by then the ships had not somehow resupplied with food, it would have been time to turn homeward again. If so, then perhaps a storm sank all four ships in the open ocean.

On the other hand, a storm may have dashed Cabot, his men, and his ships against a rockbound coast even earlier in the expedition. In 1501, the Portuguese explorer Gaspar Corte-Real found an Italian gilt sword and Venetian earrings in the possession of a Beothuk Indian in Newfoundland. It's rather sad to think of the body of John Cabot washing ashore on the land he proclaimed was the doorstep to a new world. One historian of the day wrote sneeringly that Cabot "found his new lands only in the ocean's bottom, to which he and his ships are thought to have sunk, since, after that voyage, he was never heard of more."

Whatever happened to the doomed expedition, no stampede of nations followed Cabot in other ships. Between 1498 and 1500, a few Portuguese explorers–Miguel and Gaspar Corte-Real being the most famous–visited Greenland, Labrador, and Newfoundland. Between 1501 and 1505, five English traders working as a group made voyages to Newfoundland. By 1504, French, Spanish, Portuguese, and English fishermen were crossing the ocean to catch fish on the Newfoundland banks.

But Cabot's voyages did not immediately inspire the founding of colonies in North America. In fact,

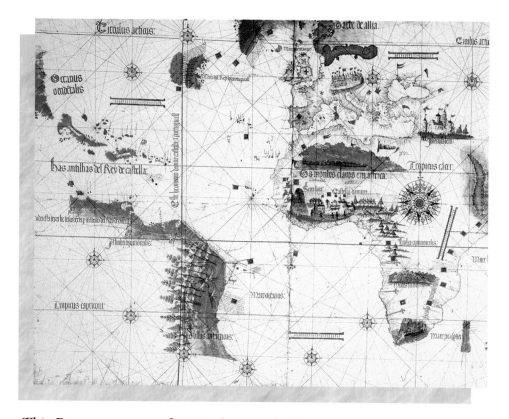

This Portuguese map of 1501 shows only the vague eastern coastline of South America and the islands of the Caribbean. John Cabot's voyages would help place North America on European maps, and would eventually lead to English colonization of the New World.

none would take hold for almost another century. What, then, is John Cabot's place in history?

Until Cabot started out in the *Matthew* in 1497, it seemed as though Spain and Portugal would take possession of the unknown lands of the New World unchallenged by any other nation. When Cabot planted the English flag on the North American continent, England took its first step in the Age of Discovery. The timid fishing expeditions that followed Cabot to Newfoundland led much later to English settlements in Virginia and New England. Likewise, the throne used Cabot's expeditions to lay claim to Canada.

Cabot also assisted a revolution in exploration and mapmaking. It gradually became clear to Europeans that Cabot had not found the lands Marco Polo had described, no more than had Christopher Columbus. Asia must lie beyond this huge, mysterious landmass to the west. Finding a way around or through it—a route later referred to as the Northwest Passage—became the goal. Over the next two centuries, such English explorers as Martin Frobisher, John Davis, and Henry Hudson would undertake the search.

Because of the Venetian merchant sailor John Cabot, fewer monster faces and other fanciful decorations appeared in the empty places on European maps. In their place, additional coastlines of an expanded world came into focus.

Chronology

500s According to legend, St. Brendan, an Irish monk, sets sail with 17 other monks on a westward voyage to spread Christianity; during their seven-year journey, they reach "the Land of Promise of the Saints," which may have been Newfoundland.

870s The Norse settle in Iceland.

982 Erik the Red, a Norseman, discovers Greenland.

985 The Norse organize a major expedition in Iceland, sail to Greenland, and establish 300 farmsteads spread throughout southeastern Greenland.

1000s The Norse build a small settlement at L'Anse aux Meadows in Newfoundland; it may have been used as a place for Norse ships to restock and be repaired.

1450s John Cabot is born in Genoa, Italy.

1471 Becomes a citizen of Venice.

1482 Marries a Venetian woman, Mattea, with whom he has three sons.

1490 Moves with his family to Valencia in Spain, perhaps because he wants to be part of Spanish plans to find a sea route to Asia.

1493 Christopher Columbus announces he has made the westward trip across the Atlantic Ocean to Asia.

1494– Cabot settles his family in England; builds support among
1495 Bristol merchants and King Henry VII to find a shorter, northern route to Asia.

1496 On March 5, King Henry VII grants official permission for Cabot and his sons to explore any lands unknown to Christians in any area except where the Spanish have claims; Cabot sets out from Bristol on his first trip, but the ship runs short of food and the weather turns bad, forcing an early return to Bristol.

1497 With a crew of 18 men, Cabot sails again from Bristol on the *Matthew* on May 20; on June 24, after a rough voyage, Cabot reaches either southern Labrador, Newfoundland, or Cape Breton Island. He explores the coastline for a month; on August 6, he sails triumphantly into Bristol.

1498 On February 3, King Henry VII grants new letters of permission for a third Cabot expedition; Cabot's third expedition, consisting of five ships and 300 men, leaves Bristol in May.

1499 Only one of Cabot's ships returns to Ireland, damaged by weather. The others never return, and Cabot is never heard from again.

Glossary

artifact–a handmade tool or ornament from a particular period or culture, or any product of human activity.

astronomer–a person who studies the stars, planets, and other objects in the sky.

boatswain–the member of a ship's crew who is responsible for taking care of the ship's hull.

bow–the front or forward part of a ship.

curragh–a wood- or wicker-framed boat covered in sewn animal hides used by medieval Irish and British sailors.

envoy–a person who represents a government or leader in dealings with another government or leader.

excavation–the process of digging to uncover something buried.

flotilla–a fleet of ships.

frontier–the farthest limits of knowledge, exploration, or settlement.

hemp–a plant with tough fibers, from which ropes can be woven.

hull–the outer frame or body of a ship.

keel–a timber on the bottom of a ship's hull that extends the entire length of the hull.

knörr–a sturdy sailing ship used especially by the Norse, or Vikings, to carry cargo.

landfall–the land first sighted on a voyage.

landform–a natural surface feature of an area of land.

mariner–a sailor.

mutiny–to rebel against the authority of a captain or commanding officer.

navigation–the science of directing the course of a seagoing vessel, and of determining its position.

pension–a fixed amount of money paid regularly to a person, usually as a reward for a period of employment or for outstanding service rendered.

pilot–a skilled sailor who is qualified to take over a ship.

saga–a heroic tale, about historic or legendary figures, that was recorded in Iceland during the 12th or 13th century; or another story that resembles the Icelandic sagas.

Scandinavia–a region of northern Europe that includes the present-day countries of Denmark, Finland, Norway, and Sweden.

spars–wooden pieces on a sailing ship, such as masts and booms, that hold sails aloft.

spices–any of various aromatic vegetable products, such as pepper or nutmeg, used to season or flavor foods. In the 15th and 16th centuries, spices were rare and highly valued by the people of Europe.

stern–the rear or back end of a ship.

whetstone–a stone used to sharpen tools or weapons.

whorl–a drum-shaped part of a spindle (which is used for spinning or weaving cloth) that helps turn the spindle.

Further Reading

Boorstin, Daniel J. *The Discoverers.* New York: Random House, 1983.

Faber, Harold. *The Discoverers of America.* New York: Scribner, 1992.

Fritz, Jean. *Around the World in a Hundred Years: From Henry the Navigator to Magellan.* New York: Putnam, 1994.

Gallagher, Jim. *The Viking Explorers.* Philadelphia: Chelsea House, 2001.

Kemp, Peter, ed. *The Oxford Companion to Ships and the Sea.* London: Oxford University Press, 1976.

Lauber, Patricia. *Who Discovered America? Mysteries and Puzzles of the New World.* New York: HarperCollins, 1992.

Martin, Steve, and Colin Sanger. *Matthew: A Voyage from the Past into the Future.* Cornwall, England: Godrevy Publications, 1996.

Morison, Samuel Eliot. *The European Discovery of America: The Northern Voyages, 500-1600 AD.* New York: Oxford University Press, 1971.

Sheaves, D. Pamela. *A Merchant's Tale: The Life and Times of John Cabot.* Newfoundland, Canada: Tuckamore Books, 1997.

Wilson, Ian. *The Columbus Myth: Did Men of Bristol Reach America Before Columbus?* Toronto: Simon & Schuster, 1991.

Picture Credits

CHARLES J. SHIELDS lives in Homewood, a suburb of Chicago, with his wife Guadalupe, an elementary school principal. He has a degree in history from the University of Illinois in Urbana-Champaign, and was chairman of the English department and the guidance department at Homewood-Flossmoor High School in Flossmoor, Illinois.

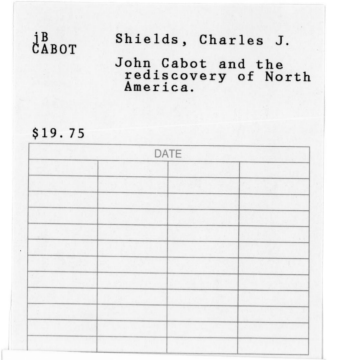

jB
CABOT

Shields, Charles J.

John Cabot and the
rediscovery of North
America.

$19.75

DATE		